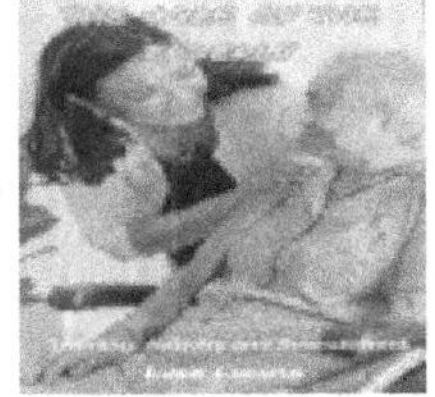

Introduction

The care sector has become an important area in the healthcare sector in recent years. The increasing demand for nursing services, particularly due to the ageing population, requires an adequate number of qualified nursing staff. Recruitment for nursing professions is therefore an important factor for the quality of nursing care and patient safety. In this essay, we will look at recruitment for the nursing professions. We will first describe and analyze the challenges of recruitment in the nursing industry. We will then look at the importance of recruitment for the quality of care and outline some solutions for recruiting nurses. Recruitment challenges: Recruitment for nursing professions is one of the biggest challenges currently facing the nursing industry. One of the main reasons for this challenge is the lack of qualified specialists. Many nurses work part-time or irregular hours, which makes it difficult to fill full-time positions. In addition, the COVID-19 pandemic has made recruitment even more difficult, as many nurses are absent due to quarantine measures or illness. Another problem is the high turnover rate of nursing staff. Many nurses leave their profession due to overwork, stress and burnout. This leads to a high demand for continuous recruitment and training to ensure the continuity of care provision. Importance of recruitment for the quality of care: Adequate recruitment is crucial for the quality of care provision. If there are not enough qualified nurses, the quality of care suffers, which can lead to a deterioration in the health and well-being of patients. This can also have a negative impact on the working conditions and well-being of nursing staff and lead to a higher turnover rate. Recruitment solutions: In order to improve recruitment for nursing professions, various solutions need to be considered. One possibility is to improve the working conditions and remuneration for nursing staff. Higher pay, better working hours and more support in coping with stress and burnout can help to encourage more people to enter and stay in the care profession. Another option is to improve the education and training of nurses.

What are nursing professions?

Caring professions are professions that focus on the care, support and nursing of people in different age groups. There are a variety of care professions, which can vary depending on the country and region. The best-known care professions include nursing specialists, geriatric nurses, nurses, home care workers and care assistants. Nursing professions generally require a high level of sensitivity and empathy towards the needs and concerns of people, especially those in a difficult situation. The most common activities performed by nursing professionals include helping with personal hygiene, feeding and mobilizing patients. They may also perform medical tasks such as administering medication or monitoring vital signs. In many cases, nursing professionals also work closely with other healthcare professions to ensure that their patients receive comprehensive care. Nursing professions are generally very demanding and require a high level of resilience. Nurses often have to work in stressful and unpredictable situations and adjust to irregular working hours. In addition, they may also experience emotionally challenging situations such as dealing with death and supporting patients in difficult situations. In order to work in a nursing profession, certain training and qualifications are usually required. These can vary depending on the profession and country. In Germany, for example, there is a training course for geriatric nurses that lasts three years and consists of a theoretical and practical part. After completing this training, geriatric nurses can work in various facilities such as retirement homes or outpatient care services. Another nursing profession in Germany is the nurse, who completes a three-year training course. Nurses work in hospitals, clinics or other healthcare facilities and care for patients with various medical needs. In recent years, many other nursing professions have also developed that focus on more specific areas, such as pediatric nursing or care for people with disabilities. Care professions are vital to society as they ensure that people who need support receive appropriate care and assistance. However, in many countries, care professions face a major challenge as there is often a lack of sufficiently qualified care workers. This can lead to an overload of existing nurses and poorer care for patients. Measures are needed to counteract this problem.

Historical development of the nursing professions

The history of the nursing profession goes back to ancient times, when the sick and injured were cared for by members of their family or by slaves. Over time, however, the nursing professions have evolved and become important pillars of the healthcare system. In the Middle Ages, the sick and injured were often cared for in monasteries and other religious institutions. Here, it was mainly nuns and monks who cared for the sick. They saw their work as part of their religious duty and carried it out without pay. In the 19th century, the first hospitals were established in which care was provided by specially trained nurses. Training often took place in practice, i.e. directly in the hospital. It was only later that special schools for nursing were founded. Florence Nightingale also played an important role in the development of the nursing profession. She was a British nurse and pioneer of modern nursing. During the Crimean War, she led a team of nurses in a military hospital and ensured that hygienic conditions were improved. She is considered one of the founders of professional nursing. Over the course of the 20th century, the nursing profession became increasingly professional. Special training courses and degree programs were developed for nurses and nursing staff. Today, training often takes place at technical colleges or universities, where prospective nurses are also taught theoretical knowledge. The demands placed on nurses have also changed over time. In the past, the main focus was on caring for and looking after sick or injured people. Today, the focus is also on preventative measures and health promotion. Nurses must be familiar with many different clinical pictures and treatment options and also be able to take into account the needs of patients with mental illnesses or disabilities. Another important step in the development of the nursing professions was the introduction of generalist nursing training. This training combines the previous training courses for nursing, pediatric and geriatric care and is intended to help meet the increasing demand for nursing staff and improve the quality of nursing care. Today, nurses work in many different areas of the healthcare sector. They work in hospitals, in outpatient care, in nursing homes or in hospice and palliative care. Nurses are also active in research and teaching today. In recent years, the importance of the nursing professions has also increased in the public eye. The coronavirus pandemic has shown how important good, professional nursing care is. They make an indispensable contribution to healthcare.

Legal basis for the nursing professions

The nursing professions are regulated by law in many countries to ensure that high-quality and safe nursing services are provided. This text deals with some of the most important legal foundations for the nursing professions. Professional laws Professional laws are laws that apply specifically to a certain professional group. In many countries, there are professional laws for care professions such as nursing, geriatric care or pediatric nursing. These laws regulate, among other things, the training and qualifications required to work as a nurse and the way in which nursing services must be provided. In Germany, for example, the Nursing Act (KrPflG) regulates the training and work of nursing staff. The Geriatric Nursing Act (AltPflG) regulates the training and work of geriatric nursing staff. Both laws precisely define the requirements for training, practicing the profession and the qualifications required to work as a nurse. Patients' rights laws Patients' rights laws regulate the rights of patients and their relatives with regard to medical treatment and care services. Many countries have patients' rights laws that also apply to the nursing professions. These laws protect the rights of patients and regulate, among other things, consent to medical treatment, the information and education of patients about their illness and treatment options, as well as the documentation and disclosure of patient data. In Germany, the Patients' Rights Act (PatRG) regulates the rights of patients and their relatives with regard to medical treatment and care services. Among other things, the law stipulates that patients have the right to comprehensive information about their illness and treatment options, that they must be involved in decisions about their treatment and that their privacy and personal rights must be protected. Professional regulations Professional regulations are ethical guidelines issued by professional associations or chambers for the nursing professions. They lay down rules for practicing the profession and serve to ensure the quality of care services and protect the rights and interests of patients. In Germany, for example, there is the Professional Code of Conduct for the Nursing Professions (BO) of the German Nursing Council. The BO contains ethical principles for practicing the profession, such as the requirement to respect human dignity and the confidentiality of patient data. It also contains rules for cooperation with other healthcare professions and for the further education and training of nursing staff.

Job profiles in nursing care

There are many different job profiles in nursing, all of which make an important contribution to the care and support of sick people or people in need of care. I will describe some of these job profiles in more detail below. Nursing specialist: The nursing specialist is a central profession in the care sector. They have three years of training and are responsible for providing nursing care to patients and residents. This includes tasks such as carrying out medical procedures, assisting with personal hygiene, administering medication and documenting nursing measures. Geriatric nurse: As a geriatric nurse, you specialize in the care and nursing of older people. The training also lasts three years and, in addition to the basics of nursing care, also provides special knowledge in gerontology, the study of ageing and the associated illnesses. Healthcare and nursing assistant: The healthcare and nursing assistant is another important occupational profile in nursing. They also have three years of training and usually work in hospitals. Their tasks include monitoring patients, carrying out medical procedures and looking after relatives. Nursing assistant: Nursing assistants usually work in geriatric care or home nursing. The training usually lasts one year and teaches basic nursing skills. The nursing assistant's tasks include assisting with personal hygiene, helping with food intake and accompanying patients to medical appointments. Nursing assistant: The nursing assistant is a job profile that is primarily used in inpatient nursing care. The training lasts one year and teaches basic nursing care, hygiene and first aid. The tasks of the nursing assistant include assisting with the mobilization of patients, providing support with personal hygiene and monitoring vital signs. Healing education nurse: The healing education nurse is a job profile that is primarily used in the care of the disabled. The training lasts three years and provides knowledge in the care and nursing of people with disabilities. The tasks of the curative education nurse include the promotion of independence and participation in social life, support during leisure activities and assistance with personal hygiene.

Areas of responsibility and activities in care

Nursing care encompasses many different areas of responsibility and activities aimed at promoting the health and well-being of patients and residents. Some of the most important areas and activities in nursing care are described below: Basic care: basic care includes activities such as washing, dressing, personal hygiene, toilet training, assistance with feeding and the application of incontinence products. These activities are often necessary to support patients in everyday activities and to maintain their physical health. Treatment care: Treatment care involves carrying out medical procedures such as administering medication, changing dressings, inserting catheters or carrying out infusions. These activities often require a high level of medical knowledge and experience. Documentation: Documentation is an important part of nursing care. It includes recording information about the patient's state of health, the implementation of care measures and the administration of medication. Accurate documentation is necessary to ensure continuity of care and to facilitate collaboration with other professionals. Counseling: Counseling is an important part of nursing care. Nursing staff advise patients and their relatives on measures to promote health and prevent illness. They provide information about the effects of certain illnesses and help with the decision for or against certain treatment options. Palliative care: Palliative care is a specialized form of care that aims to support patients with a serious illness or at the end of their lives. The nursing staff ensure a pleasant and pain-free time for the patient, promote their well-being and support their relatives. Dementia care: Dementia care includes the care of patients with dementia. The nursing staff support the patients in everyday activities and provide a structured environment that meets the patients' needs. Wound management: Wound management covers the treatment of wounds, including cleaning, disinfection and dressing changes. The nursing staff work closely with doctors and other specialists to ensure effective wound treatment. Care planning: Care planning involves the development of individual care plans for each patient. The nursing staff take into account the patient's state of health and their needs.

Qualifications and training in nursing

Nursing is an essential profession that is vital to the well-being of society. Qualifications and training are essential for a career in nursing. In this article, I will look at some of the most important qualifications and training options for nurses. Qualifications for nursing Empathy and compassion: One of the most important qualifications for nursing is the ability to have empathy and compassion for patients. It is important for nurses to be able to show understanding and empathy for patients' needs. Patience: Another important characteristic for a career in nursing is patience. Nurses must be able to work with patients who may have behavioral or cognitive impairments. Physical stamina: Caregivers often have to work long hours and lift heavy objects. It is therefore important that they have sufficient physical stamina and strength. Ability to work in a team: Nurses often have to work in teams to ensure comprehensive care for their patients. It is therefore important that they have good interpersonal and teamwork skills. Technology skills: The nursing industry is constantly evolving and nurses need to be familiar with the latest technology and electronic patient records. Training opportunities in nursing There are various training opportunities in nursing, depending on the career you want to pursue. Below are some of the most common training options: Nursing Assistant: A nursing assistant is a person who assists in the daily care of patients in hospitals, nursing homes or private homes. The training usually lasts 6-12 months and covers basic nursing skills such as personal hygiene, administering medication and helping with activities of daily living. Healthcare and nursing assistant: Training to become a healthcare and nursing assistant usually lasts three years and includes theoretical instruction and practical experience in hospitals, nursing homes and outpatient care services. Nurses are responsible for carrying out medical procedures, administering medication and monitoring patients. Geriatric nurse: Training as a geriatric nurse usually takes three years and includes theoretical instruction and practical experience in nursing homes and outpatient care services. Geriatric nurses are responsible for the care and nursing of elderly people.

Special features of the nursing professions compared to other occupational fields

The nursing professions are unique in many respects compared to other occupational fields. Some of the most important special features of the nursing professions are explained below: Human interaction: The nursing professions are primarily professions that focus on caring for people. Most other professions focus on working with objects or concepts, whereas the caring professions focus on working with people. Nurses therefore have a close relationship with their patients and are often the primary caregiver during hospitalization or recovery. Physical strain: Working in nursing often requires physical exertion, as nurses often have to lift, move and care for patients. This can lead to an increased risk of injury and strain that is not as common in other professions. Emotional stress: Working in nursing can also be emotionally stressful, as nurses are often confronted with the grief, suffering and pain of their patients. The ability to deal with these emotions while providing professional and empathetic care is an important skill in nursing. Shift work: Many nursing professions require shift work as care is needed around the clock. This can lead to sleep disturbances, exhaustion and social isolation as caregivers often work at times when other people have free time. Ongoing education: Nursing professions require ongoing education as medical and nursing practices and technologies are constantly evolving. Nurses need to keep up to date on a regular basis to provide the best possible care for their patients. Teamwork: Nursing professions require close collaboration with other nurses, physicians and other healthcare providers. The ability to work and communicate effectively as part of a team is therefore essential. Responsibility: Nurses bear a high level of responsibility for the well-being of their patients. They often have to make quick decisions and provide appropriate care to their patients, even when faced with difficult situations. This responsibility can lead to high stress levels and requires a high degree of professionalism and self-control. Ethical and moral considerations: Nurses often have to make ethical and moral considerations when making difficult decisions about the treatment of their patients. They must be able to make these decisions while respecting and honoring the rights and wishes of their patients.

The importance of the nursing profession to society

The caring professions are of vital importance to society as they look after the health and well-being of people. Nursing professions encompass a variety of activities, including assisting patients with basic care, administering medications, monitoring vital signs and administering medical treatments. In this article, we will look at the importance of nursing professions to society. First of all, nursing professions are essential to healthcare. Without qualified nurses, hospitals, clinics and care facilities could not function. Nurses play a vital role in supporting doctors and other healthcare professionals to ensure that patients receive the best possible care. They are also responsible for caring for patients who are unable to care for themselves due to illness or injury. Nurses are a bridge between patients and other healthcare professionals who are responsible for the treatment and diagnosis of illnesses and injuries. Secondly, nursing professions contribute to the prevention of disease. Nurses have an important role in recognizing signs of illness and maintaining the health of patients. By regularly monitoring vital signs such as blood pressure, heart rate and respiration, nurses can recognize early signs of illness and take appropriate action. They are also responsible for following hygiene and sterilization protocols to prevent the spread of infection. In this respect, nurses can help slow down the spread of diseases in society. Thirdly, nurses also support the social integration of patients. Many patients, especially the elderly or people with chronic diseases, often feel isolated and lonely. Caregivers can help reduce social isolation by talking to patients, listening to them and attending to their emotional needs. They can also involve family members and friends of patients in their care to provide positive social support. Fourth, nursing professions are also important to the economy. Caregivers make up a significant portion of the healthcare industry's labor force, helping to create jobs and strengthen the economy. The demand for qualified nursing staff is expected to continue to rise in the coming years due to demographic change and the increasing number of people with chronic illnesses.

The labor market for nursing staff

The labor market for nurses is a very dynamic and complex field that is influenced by various factors. Here are some important aspects that influence the labor market for nurses. Demographic change: One of the most important driving forces for the labor market for nurses is demographic change. With the ageing population, the demand for nursing staff is increasing, especially in geriatric care. In Germany, there is a constantly growing need for qualified nursing staff as the number of older people increases. Qualifications and training: Another important aspect of the labor market for nursing staff is qualifications and training. The higher the qualifications and training of a care worker, the greater their career opportunities and earning potential. In Germany, the three-year training course to become a qualified nurse is the standard. However, there are also other training options such as the two-year training course to become a nursing assistant or the academic training course to become a Bachelor of Science in Nursing. Working conditions: Working conditions are an important factor in the labor market for nursing staff. The workload in nursing is high and the profession can be physically and emotionally demanding. In order to retain nurses and attract new ones, working conditions must be improved, such as appropriate pay, working time regulations, career opportunities and a better work-life balance. Competition from other sectors: The labor market for nurses is also affected by competition from other industries. Nurses are not only employed in the healthcare sector, but can also work in other areas such as social services, childcare and care for the disabled. This leads to competition for qualified nursing staff. Technological progress: Technological progress also has an impact on the labor market for nursing staff. With the development of robots and other automated technologies, some care tasks can be automated. This leads to a decrease in demand for manual nursing work. On the other hand, technology is also opening up new opportunities, such as telemedicine, which enables nurses to care for patients remotely. Globalization: Globalization also has an impact on the labour market for nursing staff. In Germany, nurses are increasingly being recruited from other countries to meet the growing demand for nursing staff. This has led to a rise in international competition and increased competition for qualified nursing staff. Overall, it is clear that the labor market for nursing staff is very dynamic and complex.

Personnel situation in the care sector

The care sector is an important pillar of the healthcare system and plays a crucial role in the care and support of people who require assistance due to illness, age or disability. Working in the care sector requires a high degree of empathy, patience and sensitivity, but also a deep understanding of medical aspects. The staffing situation in the care sector has become one of the biggest challenges in recent years. There is a growing demand for nurses as the population ages in many countries and the use of healthcare services increases. At the same time, the supply of qualified nursing staff is limited, leading to strong competition for workers. Demographic trends, the age structure and higher demands on the quality and quantity of care have led to a tense personnel situation in the care sector in recent years. The search for qualified nursing staff is difficult due to the shortage of skilled workers, and many positions remain unfilled. As a result, existing staff often have to work overtime and are exposed to a higher workload, which leads to increased stress levels and can potentially affect the quality of patient care. Another problem in the nursing industry is the high turnover of staff, especially among new or inexperienced nurses. Due to the physical and emotional strain of the work and often inadequate working conditions, many nurses decide to change careers or move within the industry. This leads to a shortage of experienced nursing staff and increases the burden on the remaining employees. Various measures are required to improve the personnel situation in the care sector. One possibility is to create more incentives for potential nursing staff in order to make the profession more attractive. This includes higher salaries, better working conditions and improved career opportunities. Another approach is to improve education and training opportunities for nurses to ensure that they have the necessary skills and knowledge to meet the demands of the profession. The use of technology and automation can also help to reduce the workload of nurses and improve the efficiency of patient care. Examples of such technologies include digital patient records, which facilitate documentation, or robotics, which can help with simple tasks such as administering medication. Political measures are also needed to improve the staffing situation in the care sector.

Recruitment in the care sector

Recruitment in the care sector is a major challenge. The sector suffers from a considerable shortage of qualified specialists and a high fluctuation rate. This is partly due to the stress associated with working in the care sector, but also to the often inadequate working conditions and pay. In order to attract qualified specialists, it is important to develop a targeted recruitment strategy. This should pursue various approaches in order to reach a broad spectrum of potential employees. One option is to target young people who are still at the beginning of their career and are interested in training or studying in the care sector. Here it is important to emphasize the advantages and prospects of working in nursing and to dispel prejudices against the profession. Another option is to specifically recruit trained specialists who are already working in other areas of the healthcare sector. The opportunities for further training and specialization in nursing should be highlighted in order to convince potential applicants to switch to nursing. Another important starting point is the improvement of working conditions and pay. Close cooperation with employers' associations and trade unions can be helpful here in order to develop and implement solutions together. It may also be worth investing in the development of flexible working time models to appeal to employees with different needs. In addition, employer branding should also be strengthened in order to make potential applicants aware of the company and convince them to apply. The use of social media channels and the dissemination of positive testimonials from former employees can help to position the company as an attractive employer. It is also important to make the application process as simple and transparent as possible. A quick and clear response to applications and a transparent presentation of the application process can convince potential applicants to apply for a position in the care sector. Last but not least, existing employees should also be actively involved in the recruitment strategy. Referral programs, where employees can suggest potential applicants, can help to attract qualified professionals who have already been recommended by an employee and therefore already have a certain level of trust. Overall, recruitment in the care sector is a complex challenge that requires a wide range of approaches. It is important to approach potential applicants in a targeted manner in order to convince them to apply. At the same time, working conditions should be improved many times over.

Personnel development in the care sector

Personnel development in the care sector is an important topic, as it can help to ensure that employees are better qualified, perform their work more effectively and efficiently and improve patient care. The nursing industry has undergone significant change in recent years, driven by technological innovation as well as changes in legislation and demographic change. This change has emphasized the need to promote staff development in the nursing industry. Staff development can take place in various ways. One possibility is to offer employees training and further education measures to improve their skills and knowledge. Training and development can be offered in a variety of formats, from online courses and seminars to workshops and training sessions. Employees may also have the opportunity to attend conferences and trade fairs to keep up to date and exchange ideas with colleagues. Another way to develop staff is to introduce mentoring programs in which experienced employees support younger colleagues and help them develop their skills and career goals. These programs can help to promote the exchange of knowledge within the company and ensure that the knowledge and experience of older employees is not lost. Another important component of staff development is the introduction of a performance management system. Through a performance management system, employees can receive regular feedback on their performance and monitor their goals and achievements. This can help to ensure that employees remain motivated and continuously improve. Staff development in the care sector can also be supported by promoting a positive work culture and work-life balance. A positive working environment can help employees to be more satisfied and better engaged. Promoting a good work-life balance can help employees avoid stress and burnout and focus better on their work. Finally, it is important to support staff development in the care sector through appropriate pay and recognition of employees' achievements. The care sector is often associated with low pay and difficult working conditions, which can lead to employees feeling underappreciated. Appropriate pay and recognition can motivate employees to give their best and continuously improve. In summary, staff development in the care sector is crucial to ensure that employees are better qualified and can perform their work more effectively and efficiently

Employee retention in the care sector

Employee retention in the care industry is an important factor for the success of facilities and the satisfaction of employees and patients. It is well known that employee retention reduces staff turnover and therefore promotes stability and continuity in care facilities. This article outlines some ways in which employee retention can be increased in the care sector. Recognition and appreciation Employees in the care sector often work under difficult conditions and perform important work for society. Regular recognition and appreciation of their work can help employees feel valued and motivated. Various measures can be taken to achieve this, such as the introduction of employee events, the presentation of certificates or the awarding of bonuses. It is important that the recognition is tailored to the individual needs and interests of the employees. Further training and development opportunities Employees in the care sector should regularly take part in further training and courses to expand their knowledge and skills. An employer who offers this opportunity shows employees that their professional development is important to them and that they are willing to invest in their future. At the same time, employees can expand their knowledge and skills, which enables them to do their job better and more effectively. Flexibility in working time models In the care sector, flexible working time arrangements are of great importance, as work has to be done around the clock. An employer that offers different working time models gives employees the opportunity to adapt their working hours to their personal needs. This can help employees to achieve a better work-life balance and therefore be more satisfied. Health promotion Employees in the care sector are often under physical and mental strain. An employer that promotes the health of its employees shows them that it values their physical and mental health and that it is prepared to invest in their health. Various measures can be taken to this end, such as the introduction of fitness courses, massages or regular health checks. Working conditions are an important factor in employee satisfaction. An employer who ensures that the working conditions meet the requirements of the employees can increase employee loyalty. Various measures can be taken to this end, such as the provision of modern work equipment or the creation of pleasant working spaces.

Working conditions in the care sector

The care sector is one of the most important and at the same time one of the most challenging sectors in today's working world. Working conditions in the care sector are therefore of great importance, as they can directly influence the quality of care and the well-being of employees. The care sector is characterized by a high workload and a high level of responsibility. Staff are often on duty around the clock to ensure that those in need of care receive the support and care they require. The workload can therefore be very heavy, which can lead to high levels of stress. Another problem in the care sector is the shortage of skilled workers. Many facilities struggle to find and retain qualified staff. This can lead to high staff turnover and a lack of continuity in care. An important aspect of working conditions in the care sector is pay. Salaries in the care sector are often low compared to other sectors with similar responsibilities and workloads. This can lead to employees opting for other sectors or having to change jobs due to financial difficulties. Another challenge is the working hours. Many employees in the care industry work shifts, which can lead to irregular working hours and a lack of time off. Shift work can also lead to work-life balance issues, as it can be difficult to see family and friends or pursue personal interests. In addition to this, working in the care industry can also be physically and mentally demanding. Employees are often physically active and frequently have to lift and carry heavy loads. The work can also be emotionally stressful, as it can be difficult to distance oneself from the fates of those in need of care and maintain an emotional distance. Various measures are needed to improve working conditions in the care sector. Better pay and working conditions can help to attract and retain qualified employees. A better work-life balance can also help employees to stay in the care sector for longer. Another important measure is the promotion of further training and development opportunities for employees. This can help employees to develop professionally and improve their skills and knowledge. This can also help to keep employees motivated and committed to their work. In addition, it is important to regularly review and evaluate working conditions in the care sector to ensure that they meet the needs of employees and those in need of care. This should also include employee participation in decision-making processes and the involvement of trade unions and interest groups.

Working time models in the care sector

Working time models in the care sector can vary greatly depending on the type of care facility and the position of the employee. In general, however, there are various types of working time models that are common in the care sector. This article explains and discusses the most important models. Full-time position A full-time position is the classic employment model in the care sector. A full-time employee usually works 38.5 to 40 hours per week and receives a fixed monthly salary. This model offers employees a high level of job security and stability, as they have a fixed number of hours and a fixed salary. However, it can also be difficult to achieve a good work-life balance, as full-time employees often have to work overtime and often have to work weekends or public holidays. Part-time position A part-time position is an alternative to a full-time position and offers employees more flexibility. Part-time employees work fewer hours per week than full-time employees, usually between 20 and 30 hours. They receive a salary that is proportional to their working hours. Part-time employment is a good option for employees who have other commitments, such as family, studies or other work. However, part-time employees often have less job security and stability than full-time employees. Shift work Shift work is very common in the care industry, as many care facilities are open around the clock. Shift work can be a good way to achieve a work-life balance as employees often have days off and flexible working hours. Working hours are divided into shifts, often consisting of 8 to 12 hours. Shifts can include day or night shifts, weekend or public holiday shifts. Shift workers usually receive bonuses for night and weekend work. Flexitime Flexitime is a flexible working time model that allows employees to determine their own working hours within a certain period of time. For example, an employee can work between 6 a.m. and 8 p.m. as long as he or she completes the required number of hours each day. Flexitime offers employees great flexibility in planning their working lives and can be a good option for employees who need to coordinate their work with other commitments such as family, studies or other work. However, flexitime does require a certain amount of discipline and self-organization from employees. On-call duty On-call duty means that employees must be available outside their regular working hours to work in an emergency. This form of working time is often common in the care sector, as many facilities are open around the clock. Employees on call usually receive additional remuneration and generally have to respond to a request within a certain period of time.

Remuneration models in the care sector

There are various remuneration models used by employers and employees in the care sector. These models differ in the amount of the salary and the conditions under which it is paid. Some of these models are explained below. Collective agreement The collective agreement is an agreement between employers and trade unions that regulates pay and working conditions. The collective agreement is usually valid for a specific industry or a specific company. The advantage of a collective agreement is that wages and working conditions are standardized for all employees and there are usually clear rules on what is to be paid for overtime, night work or work on public holidays. The trade unions campaign for higher wages and better working conditions in collective bargaining. Hourly wage With hourly wages, the salary is calculated based on the number of hours worked. The salary is therefore directly dependent on the number of hours worked. Hourly wages are generally common for unskilled or part-time jobs. However, there are also care workers who are paid by the hour, for example in outpatient care services or 24-hour care. Salary according to experience Some employers pay a higher salary to employees who have more experience in the care sector. These employees usually have more responsibility and can take on more difficult tasks. A higher salary can be a motivation for employees to continue their education and improve their skills.

Performance-related salary A performance-related salary is based on an employee's individual performance. It is usually determined by target agreements and depends on whether the employee has achieved their targets. A performance-related salary can be a motivation for employees to improve and increase their performance. Salary by qualification Some employers pay a higher salary to employees who have a higher qualification. These employees have usually completed higher education and have more specialized knowledge. A higher salary can be a motivation for employees to continue their education and improve their qualifications. Salary according to responsibility Some employers pay a higher salary to employees who have a higher level of responsibility. This applies in particular to employees in management positions who are responsible for the management of care facilities or care departments. A higher salary can be a motivation for employees to take their responsibilities seriously and to develop themselves further. Bonus payments Some employers offer bonus payments to motivate employees. These can be based on individual or collective performance.

Labor law regulations for nursing staff

Nurses are essential in today's society and their work is of great importance to the well-being of patients and residents in care facilities. This article will explain the employment regulations for nursing staff. Employment contract The employment contract is the basis for the employment relationship between the nurse and the employer. It regulates the most important points such as working hours, place of work, remuneration, vacation and notice periods. The employment contract should always be concluded in writing. Working hours The working hours of nursing staff are regulated by law. It may not exceed 48 hours per week. A rest period of at least 11 hours must be guaranteed within 24 hours. However, working hours may be regulated differently within the framework of collective agreements or company regulations. Remuneration The remuneration of nursing staff is generally regulated by collective agreements. There are various collective agreements for geriatric and nursing care. Remuneration depends on the experience and qualifications of the nurse and the region in which they work. However, at least the statutory minimum wage must be paid. Vacation Nursing staff are entitled to paid vacation. The statutory minimum vacation entitlement is 24 working days per year. However, collective agreements or company regulations may provide for more vacation days. Termination The employment relationship can be terminated by either party with a period of notice. The notice period depends on the duration of the employment relationship. As a rule, it is four weeks to the end of the month for nursing staff. However, there are also collective bargaining or company regulations that may differ. Job security Nursing staff are entitled to a secure job. The employer is obliged to provide a safe working environment and to take measures to protect the health of nursing staff. This also includes adequate work equipment and a sufficient number of staff. Further training Nursing staff have the opportunity to undergo further training and improve their qualifications. The employer is obliged to offer and promote further training. Working time accounts Working time accounts are generally used to make working hours more flexible. Nursing staff can accumulate overtime in a working time account and reduce it at a later date. However, the use of working time accounts must be agreed with the employer. In the event of illness, nursing staff are entitled to continued remuneration from the employer. The duration of continued remuneration is regulated by law.

Health management in the care sector

Health management in the care sector is an important aspect for both employees and employers. In this article, we will look at the challenges of health management in the care industry and discuss some best practices that employees and employers can adopt to promote health and wellbeing in the workplace. Health management challenges in the care industry The care industry is one of the most demanding industries in terms of employee health. Here are some of the challenges faced by employees and employers in the care industry: Physical strain: Care workers often have to carry heavy loads and move in awkward positions, which can lead to injuries and musculoskeletal disorders. Mental stress: Working in the care industry can be very stressful and can lead to burnout, depression and other mental illnesses. Infection risks: Care workers are at high risk of contracting infectious diseases, especially in times of pandemics. Working time regulations: Work in the care industry can be very long and irregular, which can lead to lack of sleep and other health problems. Health management practices in the care industry Despite these challenges, there are best practices that employees and employers can adopt to promote health and wellbeing in the workplace. Ergonomics: Employers should ensure that working conditions are designed to minimize physical strain. This includes, for example, the use of ergonomic aids, training employees in safe working procedures and regular inspections of working conditions by specialists. Stress management: Workers should have access to stress management programs to better withstand the mental stresses of the workplace. This includes, for example, relaxation exercises, cognitive behavioral therapy and counseling services. Infection control: Employers should ensure safe working conditions that support infection control. This includes, for example, regular disinfection, training in hygiene measures and the provision of protective equipment. Working time regulations: Employers should strive to make working time arrangements as flexible as possible to minimize the burden on employees. This includes, for example, implementing working time models that make it easier to reconcile work and family life and taking into account the individual needs of employees.

Mental stress and burnout in the care sector

The care sector is known for its demanding work and the associated mental stress. Working in the care sector requires a high degree of empathy, compassion and patience. At the same time, nursing staff are often confronted with difficult situations, such as the death of patients, family conflicts or excessive demands on relatives. These stresses can lead to nursing staff suffering from burnout symptoms. Burnout is a state of emotional exhaustion, depersonalization and reduced performance that often occurs in people who work in professionally demanding environments. In the care industry, burnout can be common due to long working hours, high workloads, difficult working conditions and emotional stress. One of the main causes of burnout in the care industry is overwork. Nurses often work long shifts that are both physically and emotionally demanding. They have to care for many patients at the same time and adapt to their needs. This can lead to nurses feeling that they do not have enough time for each patient and feel overwhelmed. Another cause of burnout in the care sector is emotional stress. Nurses often have to deal with traumatic events, such as the death of patients or dealing with aggressive or disoriented patients. These experiences can lead to emotional exhaustion and cause nurses to distance themselves and alienate themselves from their patients. In addition to the direct stresses of nursing work, factors such as inadequate support, lack of resources and a poor working environment can also contribute to nurses feeling stressed and overwhelmed. If nurses feel that their work is not valued or that they do not receive enough support, this can lead to them feeling drained and frustrated. To prevent or treat caregiver burnout, employers need to take steps to reduce stress in the workplace. This includes providing adequate resources, support for difficult tasks and creating a positive work environment. Employers can also provide training and education to prepare caregivers for difficult situations and give them tools to cope with stress and strain. For nurses themselves, there are also steps they can take to prevent or treat burnout. These include looking after their own physical and emotional health by taking regular breaks, getting enough sleep, eating healthily and exercising.

Dealing with patients and relatives in nursing care

Dealing with patients and relatives in nursing is an essential part of the work of nursing staff. It requires a high degree of empathy, communication skills, patience and understanding in order to build and maintain a positive and respectful relationship. In this text, I will explain some important points that nurses should keep in mind when working with patients and relatives. Firstly, it is important that caregivers take time to understand the needs and wishes of the patient and their loved ones. Every person is unique and has individual needs and requirements that need to be taken into account. It therefore makes sense for nursing staff to seek out conversations and ask patients and relatives questions to find out what is important to them and how they can be supported. Another important aspect is respecting the patient's privacy. Everyone has the right to privacy and confidential treatment. It is therefore important that caregivers respect the patient's privacy and ensure that no unwanted persons are present during care applications. Caregivers should also ensure that any confidential information they learn during care remains confidential. Positive and respectful communication is also very important when working with patients and family members. Caregivers should always strive to speak clearly and understandably to avoid misunderstandings. They should also ensure that they listen to and respond to the needs of the patient and their relatives. Positive and respectful communication can help the patient feel comfortable and build trust in the caregiver. The needs and requirements of relatives should also be taken into account. Relatives often play an important role in the care of patients and can be a valuable source of support for the patient. It is important that nurses understand the needs and requirements of relatives and work with them to ensure that the patient receives the best possible care. In some cases, it may also be necessary to have difficult conversations with patients and relatives. This may be the case, for example, if the patient's health is deteriorating or if difficult decisions need to be made. Nurses should prepare themselves for having difficult conversations by informing themselves in advance and playing through possible scenarios. It is important that nurses communicate sensitively but also directly and clearly in such situations.

Communication in nursing care

Communication in nursing is one of the most important skills a nurse should have. Good communication can help to improve the relationship between the patient and the nurse and speed up recovery. This text explains 600 words about the importance of communication in nursing, the different types of communication and some best practices for improving communication in nursing. Importance of communication in nursing Communication is a fundamental part of nursing. A good nurse must be able to communicate effectively with patients, family members, physicians and other healthcare professionals. Poor communication can lead to misunderstandings and errors that can delay the patient's recovery. Good communication, on the other hand, can help gain the patient's trust and promote cooperation. Types of communication in nursing There are different types of communication in nursing, including Verbal communication: this type of communication involves the spoken word. It is important to speak clearly and concisely so that the patient understands what is being said. Non-verbal communication: This type of communication includes body language, gestures, facial expressions and eye contact. Non-verbal communication can be just as important as verbal communication and can help to improve trust and rapport with the patient. Written communication: This type of communication includes anything that is recorded in writing, such as notes, reports and patient records. It is important that written communication is clear and concise to avoid misunderstandings. Best practices for improving communication in nursing Listening: One of the most important methods for improving communication in nursing is listening. The care professional should take time to listen to the patient and understand their concerns and issues. Use clear language: The care professional should use clear language and avoid technical terms that the patient may not understand. Use non-verbal communication: The care professional should also use non-verbal communication to show the patient that he or she is paying attention and understands him or her. Show empathy: It is important to show empathy and show the patient that you care about him or her. Take your time: The nurse should take time to listen to the patient.

Hygiene management in the care sector

Hygiene management plays a very important role in the care sector. Hygiene is of great importance as it helps to prevent or minimize the transmission of diseases and infections. The care sector covers various areas such as hospitals, nursing homes, outpatient care facilities and also care for patients at home. Hygiene management must be observed in all of these areas. Effective hygiene management starts with staff education and training. Nursing staff must be informed and trained about the importance of hygiene in care. Staff should be informed about the current standards and guidelines that apply to the care sector. Regular training and education can help to keep staff knowledge and skills up to date. Another important aspect of hygiene management is the use of appropriate protective clothing. Staff should wear appropriate gloves, protective clothing, masks and other protective equipment to minimize the transmission of disease and infection. Protective equipment should also be changed and cleaned regularly to ensure its effectiveness. Hand hygiene is another important aspect of hygiene management. Staff should wash their hands regularly and thoroughly to minimize the transmission of disease and infection. It is important that staff are also educated on the correct hand washing technique to ensure it is effective. Cleaning and disinfecting surfaces and objects is another important aspect of hygiene management in the care industry. Surfaces and objects touched by patients should be cleaned and disinfected regularly to minimize the transmission of disease and infection. The cleaning agents and disinfectants should comply with the standards and guidelines of the care sector. Another important aspect of hygiene management is the monitoring of infections and illnesses. Staff should recognize symptoms of infection and illness in patients and take appropriate action to prevent the spread. Staff should also be able to isolate patients to minimize the transmission of disease and infection. The care industry should also have an effective waste disposal policy. Waste should be disposed of properly to minimize the transmission of disease and infection. Staff should be educated on the proper disposal of waste to ensure it is effective. Another important aspect of hygiene management is the monitoring of water quality.

Quality management in the care sector

Quality management in the care industry is vital to ensure that patients and residents receive high quality care. It encompasses all aspects of the care process, including the assessment of the patient or resident's needs, the planning and implementation of care, the monitoring and evaluation of outcomes, and the continuous improvement of processes and the quality of care. Compliance with legal and regulatory requirements plays an important role in quality management in care. There are a variety of rules and regulations set by health authorities and other regulatory bodies. These include, for example, the qualifications of nursing staff, hygiene and safety standards, documentation and reporting, the administration of medication and the implementation of infection prevention procedures. Another important aspect of quality management in care is patient or resident satisfaction. Patient or resident satisfaction is a key measure of the quality of care. It is therefore important to obtain feedback from them and take their opinions and needs into account. This can be done through surveys, interviews and other assessment methods. Based on this feedback, care facilities can improve their processes and services and ensure that the needs of patients or residents are met. The implementation of quality assurance measures is another important aspect of quality management in care. These measures include reviewing care protocols and policies, training caregivers in the latest techniques and procedures, monitoring care processes and recording care outcomes. Through these measures, care facilities can ensure that their processes and services meet the highest standards and are continuously improved. An important part of quality management in care is the involvement of stakeholders. These can be nursing staff, patients, residents, relatives, regulatory authorities and others. Involving these groups in the quality management process can help to ensure that their needs and opinions are taken into account and that care facilities can respond to their concerns. Another important aspect of quality management in care is continuous improvement. This means that care facilities constantly monitor and evaluate their processes and performance and make improvements based on these evaluations.

Digitalization in the care sector

Digitalization has also become increasingly important in the care sector. The opportunities offered by digitalization are manifold and can make work in care considerably easier. This text explains some of the most important aspects of digitalization in care in more detail. One of the most important opportunities offered by digitization in care is electronic documentation. Instead of recording all data on paper as before, all important information can now be recorded and stored electronically. This not only saves time and space, but also enables better and faster data analysis. Electronic documentation can also help to minimize errors and improve the quality of care. Another important aspect of digitalization in care is telemedicine. Here, technical devices and applications are used to improve medical care. For example, doctors and nurses can use video conferencing to communicate with patients in order to respond quickly and effectively to questions or problems. It is also possible to monitor vital signs or carry out remote treatments. Telemedicine can improve patient care and reduce the workload of nursing staff. Another important aspect of digitalization in care is the use of care apps. These are applications for smartphones or tablets that have been specially developed for use in care. These apps can help to optimize workflows and facilitate communication between nursing staff. Nursing apps can also simplify the monitoring of patients or the administration of medication. In addition to telemedicine and care apps, there are also numerous other ways in which digitalization can support care. For example, smart care beds or sensors in the room can help patients feel safer and more comfortable. The use of robots in care is also increasingly being discussed. These are special robots that can take over certain tasks in care, such as monitoring vital signs or carrying out simple treatments. Despite all the advantages offered by digitalization in care, there are also some critical voices. Some fear, for example, that the use of robots in care could lead to the interpersonal component being lost. Others fear that the use of technology could distract nursing staff from their actual task. However, it is important to emphasize that digitalization in care is not intended as a replacement for human attention and care, but as a supplement.

Future prospects for the care professions

The care sector is one of the fastest growing industries in the world and is expected to grow even further in the coming years. With an ageing population, the rise of chronic diseases and an increasing demand for quality care, the future prospects for the care professions are very promising. Some of the future prospects for the care professions are described below: Technology will play a greater role: The care sector will become increasingly technology-oriented. New technologies such as robotics, artificial intelligence and virtual reality will be used in nursing to improve the quality of care and make working conditions easier for nursing staff. Telemedicine solutions will also be increasingly used to monitor patients remotely and help them manage their health. Demand for specialized nurses: The care industry will also require specialized caregivers to meet the needs of an aging population. Geriatrics, palliative care and dementia care are areas that are expected to continue to grow. In addition, there will be a need for professionals who specialize in specific diseases and conditions, such as diabetes, cancer and cardiovascular disease. Improved training opportunities: Training opportunities for nurses will be improved. There will be more financial support for nurse training and training will be increasingly digitized. New teaching methods such as simulations and virtual reality will also be used to improve the training of nurses. Increased demand for nurses: The nursing industry is expected to continue to grow in the coming years, which will lead to an increase in demand for nurses. There will be more career opportunities and promotion prospects in nursing, which will lead to a higher number of nurses and better trained nurses. Care in the home: An increasing number of patients will be cared for at home in the future as the concept of care changes and technology supports care. This means that nurses will be increasingly deployed in the home environment and care will be tailored to the needs of the individual. More autonomy for care workers: In the future, care workers will have greater autonomy and will be able to make more decisions independently. This means that carers will be able to make individual decisions and play a greater role in shaping care.

International comparison of the nursing professions

The nursing professions are an important part of the healthcare system in many countries. This article provides an international comparison of the nursing professions in different countries. In particular, the training, working conditions and workload of nursing staff are examined. Training Training for the nursing profession differs from country to country. In some countries, there are special training courses for nursing, geriatric and child care. In other countries, all areas are combined into one training program. In many countries, training for the nursing profession is possible at Bachelor level. In other countries, there is only training at diploma level or a comparable qualification. In some countries, training is also linked to a specific professional qualification, such as in Germany, where training as a nursing specialist is only possible with an intermediate school leaving certificate and completed training as a healthcare and nursing assistant, geriatric nurse or pediatric nurse. Working conditions Working conditions for nurses also vary from country to country. In some countries, nurses are well paid and have good working conditions, while in others the opposite is the case. In many countries, there is a shortage of skilled nursing staff, which can lead to overwork and stress. In some countries, there are also special working time regulations for care workers to reduce their workload. Workload The workload for nurses is an important factor influencing their job satisfaction and health. In some countries, nurses have a high workload due to staff shortages and a high workload. In other countries, there are special working time regulations to reduce the workload. In some countries, there are also special programs to promote the health of nurses to help them stay healthy and better manage their work. In summary, it can be said that the nursing professions are an important part of the healthcare system in many countries. However, the training, working conditions and workload for nurses vary from country to country. In some countries there are special programs to promote the health of nurses, while in other countries the focus is on workload and working conditions. Some countries also have special working time regulations for nurses to reduce their workload. Despite the differences, however, all countries have one thing in common: the need for qualified and committed nurses to ensure high-quality care for patients.

Outlook for the future development of the nursing sector

The care sector is one of the fastest growing industries in the world. With the ageing population and the rise in chronic diseases, the demand for high-quality care is becoming ever greater. In this outlook, I would like to highlight some of the trends and challenges that the care industry will face in the future. Technology in care: Technological innovations such as telemedicine, virtual care, robotics and artificial intelligence will play an important role in the provision of care in the future. These technologies can improve efficiency, reduce costs and increase the quality of care. Staff shortage: The lack of qualified nursing staff is becoming a major problem in the industry. It is becoming increasingly difficult to find and retain trained staff. The introduction of technology in the care sector can help to alleviate the labor shortage by relieving and supporting care staff. Outpatient care: The demand for outpatient care will increase in the future. Patients want to stay at home longer and meet their care needs at home. Outpatient care will therefore play an important role in the provision of care. Preventive care: The emphasis on preventive care will increase in the future. With an ageing population and an increase in chronic diseases, prevention and early detection of illness will become more important. The care industry will increasingly focus on improving health and quality of life rather than just treating illness. New care models: New care models such as care in communities and integrated care will become more important in the future. These models aim to improve collaboration between different healthcare providers and optimize care for patients.

Challenges in the care sector

The care industry is one of the most important industries there is, as it plays a crucial role in supporting people who need assistance. While the industry offers a variety of benefits, there are also numerous challenges that must be overcome to ensure the quality of care and meet the needs of patients. Some of the key challenges facing the care industry are outlined below. Shortage of skilled staff: One of the biggest problems in the care sector is the lack of qualified nursing staff. There is a great need for nursing staff to meet the increasing demand for services. Competition for qualified staff is fierce and wages can be low, resulting in many professionals leaving the industry or being unwilling to enter the care sector. Digitalization has found its way into the care industry and can be a great help in automating processes and simplifying workflows. However, not all employees are familiar with the latest technology and need to be trained. In addition, the cost of introducing new technologies in the care sector is high, which poses a challenge. Demographic change: Demographic trends in many countries around the world mean that there are more and more older people who are dependent on care. This poses an enormous challenge for the care sector, as it is difficult to find enough staff to care for the growing number of patients. This also has an impact on the financing of care. Financing: Financing care is another challenge, as the cost of care is rising and income from state subsidies and insurance is not always sufficient to cover the costs. The care sector is dependent on finding alternative sources of funding in order to maintain the quality of care. Quality management: The care sector faces the challenge of continuously improving the quality of care. This requires effective quality management to ensure that the quality of care is constantly monitored and improved. This also includes the development of standards and guidelines as well as the training of nursing staff. Challenges when working with patients: Working in the care sector requires a great deal of empathy, patience and understanding. Nurses often have to work with difficult patients who suffer from dementia, depression or other mental illnesses. They also need to be able to care for patients from different cultural backgrounds, which brings additional challenges.

New methods to recruit nursing staff

The care industry is known to be one of the most demanding and important industries in today's society. It plays a crucial role in caring for the elderly and patients who need support due to illness or injury. In recent years, however, the industry has suffered from a shortage of qualified professionals. Recruiting care staff is a lengthy and often difficult process. In this article, we will look at some of the latest methods used by companies and organizations to attract qualified caregivers. Social media: An essential part of any modern recruitment strategy is the use of social media. Companies use platforms such as Facebook, Twitter and LinkedIn to post their job openings and reach potential candidates. In addition, social media can be used to engage with prospects and give them a better understanding of the company and its culture. Virtual job fairs: In the past, it was common for companies to attend job fairs at universities and other institutions to recruit nurses. Nowadays, however, it is possible to organize virtual job fairs. These allow applicants to get in touch with the company and learn more about the jobs on offer without having to leave home. Employee Referral Programs: Employee referral programs are another way to attract qualified nursing staff. Companies offer incentives to their employees if they successfully recruit a new caregiver to the company. This can take the form of cash bonuses or other benefits. Mobile recruiting: More and more people are using their mobile devices to search for jobs. Companies can develop mobile applications that allow candidates to search job ads and apply directly from their cell phones. More flexible working conditions: Some companies have started to offer more flexible working conditions to attract skilled professionals. This can take the form of telecommuting or flexible working hours. Building relationships with educational institutions: Companies can build relationships with schools, universities and other educational institutions to identify potential candidates early on. This can be achieved through internships, mentoring programs and other initiatives.

Personalized outreach: Companies can use personalization technology to reach out to potential candidates. This can take the form of personalized emails, advertisements and other marketing materials tailored to the specific interests and needs of applicants. Improved career development: Some companies offer career development opportunities and training to their employees.

Conclusion and recommendations for action

The care sector is an important industry that looks after the welfare and care of people who need support due to age, illness or disability. However, the care sector faces numerous challenges, such as a shortage of qualified professionals, an increase in demand for care services and a lack of funding and resources. This summary identifies the most important challenges facing the care sector and presents recommendations for action to meet these challenges. Challenges in the care sector The care sector will face many challenges in the coming years. A large proportion of these are due to demographic change. The number of older people in society is increasing, and with it the number of people who are dependent on care. This means that the demand for care services is increasing, while at the same time the shortage of qualified professionals in the sector is growing. Another problem is the financial pressure on the care industry, particularly in the public sector, which makes it more difficult to provide sufficient resources to cope with the growing demand for care services. Recommendations for action To address these challenges, various measures need to be taken to improve the quality of care and ensure that sufficient resources are available to meet the growing demand. Invest in the education and training of nursing staff: The care sector must invest in the education and training of nursing staff to ensure that sufficient qualified professionals are available. This includes the introduction of incentives to attract young people to a career in the care sector. Improving working conditions: Improving working conditions in the care sector is an important factor in attracting and retaining qualified professionals in the long term. This includes the introduction of more flexible working time models, appropriate salaries and recognition of the work of care workers. Promoting technology and innovation: Technology and innovation can make an important contribution to improving the quality and efficiency of care. Examples of this include the introduction of telemedicine, intelligent care systems and automated care models. Increased funding: In order to cope with the growing demand for care services, the care sector must be adequately funded. This also includes the introduction of incentives for private investors to invest in the care sector.

Imprint

Luna Ludwig
Am Anger 3
06869 Coswig
Germany
Luna-Publishing.de